YOURS TRULY

First published in 2025 by OH
An Imprint of HEADLINE PUBLISHING GROUP LIMITED

1

Disclaimer:
All trademarks, copyright, quotations, company names, registered names, products, characters, logos and catchphrases used or cited in this book are the property of their respective owners. This book has not been licensed, approved, sponsored, or endorsed by Ariana Grande.

Cataloguing in Publication Data is available from the British Library

ISBN 978-1-03542-290-6

Compiled and written by: Malcolm Croft
Editorial: Saneaah Muhammad
Designed and typeset in Avenir by: Stephen Cary
Project manager: Russell Porter
Production: Rachel Burgess
Printed and bound in China

FSC www.fsc.org MIX Paper | Supporting responsible forestry FSC® C104740

Headline's policy is to use papers that are natural, renewable and recyclable products and made from wood grown in well-managed forests and other controlled sources. The logging and manufacturing processes are expected to conform to the environmental regulations of the country of origin.

HEADLINE PUBLISHING GROUP LIMITED
An Hachette UK Company
Carmelite House, 50 Victoria Embankment, London EC4Y 0DZ

The authorised representative in the EEA is Hachette Ireland, 8 Castlecourt Centre, Castleknock Road, Castleknock, Dublin 15, D15 YF6A, Ireland

www.headline.co.uk www.hachette.co.uk

YOURS TRULY

THE LITTLE GUIDE TO ARIANA GRANDE

UNOFFICIAL AND UNAUTHORIZED

CONTENTS

INTRODUCTION

Ariana Grande is the voice of her generation – and what an incredible voice it is. Today, and for the past decade or so, Ariana has remained one of the most prolific and passionate singers on the planet, releasing a staggering symphony of critically and commercially acclaimed studio albums and singles, each one an impressive progression on what came before.

Hailing from Boca Raton, Florida, and born in 1993, Ariana's *victorious* path to TV, music and film glory has been a phenomenal, if sometimes hellish, ride, full of intense highs and severe lows, and with more than her unfair share of tragedy, grief, controversies, fear and false starts. She may have experienced her first taste of fame as a 15-year-old Broadway actress in 2008 and blossomed on screen as Cat Valentine in the show *Victorious*, but it was as the R&B and pop singer extraordinaire that Ariana Grande truly discovered her destiny. In ten years and seven albums, this kind-hearted princess has possessed the charts with a string of R&B bangers, pop ballads and trap beats, each one energizing Ariana's loyal fanbase (the Arianators), each one a modern classic. Right now, Ariana Grande rules the world. And thank God she does. She's precisely what we need.

This grand little guide is the ultimate celebration of Ari; a tiny tome packed with her greatest words of wit and wisdom (of which there are a lot – she's got a wicked sense of humour). As compact as the singer herself – despite her last name, ironically, meaning large – this pocket-sized, petite compendium delves deep into Ariana's still-rising stardom and throws a bright eternal spotlight on what makes her shine. Enjoy!

CHAPTER ONE

ARI FROM BOCA

Ariana's childhood was as blessed, and as cursed, as the plots of the fantasy and horror movies she watched, and idolized, as she grew up.

Her parents' divorce may have detonated her fun-filled Floridan family life when she was only eight, but for Ariana, an ordinary, normal life was never part of the plan anyway...

“I loved growing up in Boca Raton, it was a great place to grow up. I grew up going to the beach all the time. I started doing theatre in a family community theatre there. I was eight years old when I started – performing *The Wizard of Oz* and *Beauty and the Beast* and all those cute plays. I played Annie, it was my first role, and then I just never stopped! When I was 13 I started taking it seriously.”

Ariana, on her Florida hometown, interview with Lauren Nostro, *Complex*, August 27, 2013.

"

I was singing in the car with my mom. I was about four or five or something. My mom was like 'Do that again.' And she was like 'Oh my God, you can really sing!' I thought everyone was a singer. I thought it was normal!

"

Ariana, on the moment when her mother Joan realized her daughter could sing, interview with Davina McCall, *An Evening with Ariana Grande*, November 1, 2018.

"

I was a very weird little girl. I always wanted to have skeleton face paint on or be wearing a Freddy Krueger mask, and I would carry a hockey stick around.

"

Ariana, on her childhood, and being "dark and deranged", interview with Lizzy Goodman, *Billboard*, August 15, 2014.

"I am a workaholic. It is the thing I know how to do best. I've been working straight since I made my Broadway debut at the age of 14."

Ariana, on her prolific body of work and her love of her job, interview with Giles Hattersley, *Vogue*, August 14, 2018.

Ariana's first gig, as confirmed by her on *The Tonight Show Starring Jimmy Fallon*, was performing America's national anthem, "The Star Spangled Banner", at a sold-out Florida Panthers hockey game in 2001.

She was just eight years old! The YouTube video of this moment has more than 10 million views.

"My family was the stereotypical poker-playing, loud, friendly, food-shoving, loving, Italian family."

Ariana, on her Italian American upbringing, interview with Joe La Puma, *Complex*, November 5, 2013.

"I auditioned for [the musical] *13*, and out of thousands of kids they picked me! I came to New York with my best friend [Aaron Simon Gross]; we had grown up together doing musical theatre since we were seven years old. The cast was 13 kids and out of 13 kids, we both got cast, out of thousands of kids. How is that even possible? It was insane."

Ariana, on getting cast for *13*, a Broadway production, with her childhood friend from Boca Raton, interview with Lauren Nostro, *Complex*, August 27, 2013.

“

To me the idea of being a role model is just being unapologetically yourself. That can be me simply dressing sexier on some days and more conservatively on other days because that's how I wake up feeling. I believe in authenticity.

”

Ariana, on being true to herself, and being a role model, interview with Craig McLean, *Daily Telegraph*, October 14, 2014.

“

I come from a strong, loud Italian family. We don’t take shit from anybody.

”

Ariana, when asked if she would ever be forced into doing something she didn’t want to do for her music, interview with Craig McLean, *Daily Telegraph*, October 14, 2014.

“

Growing up, I was listening to Whitney Houston’s *The Bodyguard* soundtrack all the time, as well as a lot of Judy Garland and oldies, and divas. I just loved music; I was just always writing cute songs with GarageBand too. Music was always such a massive part of my life, it’s my passion.

”

Ariana, on her childhood playlists and earliest songwriting attempts, interview with Lauren Nostro, *Complex*, August 27, 2013.

“I would stand in front of the TV and mimic her body movements. I was always fascinated. She carried herself in a way that was so protected and soft and Judy.”

Ariana, on her biggest singing influence, and idol, Judy Garland, interview with Giles Hattersley, *Vogue*, August 14, 2018.

“My nonna is the best cook in the world. She made the best marinara sauce ever. Every Christmas she’d make zeppole and spiedini and everything Italian. Then I grew up and changed my diet completely. Now, I only eat salmon, vegetables, and fruits – super healthy.”

Ariana, on no longer enjoying the delicious treats of her family’s Sicilian heritage, interview with Joe La Puma, *Complex*, November 5, 2013.

“

My mom is a CEO and owns a company that manufactures communications equipment for the Marines and the Navy. So she’s not really the housewife type, if you get what I’m saying.

”

Ariana, on the "most badass, independent woman you'll ever meet – not the cookies-in-the-oven type" mother, Joan, interview with Joe La Puma, *Complex*, November 5, 2013.

“

That was very hard as a young girl when my parents got divorced. Being in the middle of it was so stressful. And of course being made up of both of them – I was like, 'Hey, if they both dislike each other's attributes so much, what am I to like about me? I'm made from these two people and I'm caught in the middle of all this fighting.' It was traumatic.

”

Ariana, on her parents' divorce, aged eight, interview with Craig McLean, *Daily Telegraph*, October 14, 2014.

"I called 411, and I got through by some miracle and I said, 'Hi I would like to audition to be on a show, your pick', and they were like 'How old are you?' and I was like, 'Don't worry about it!'"

Ariana, on manifesting her destiny and the time she called Universal Studios, Orlando, Florida, and asked to audition to be on a Universal TV show*, *The Tonight Show Starring Jimmy Fallon*, November 5, 2021.

* She was just four years old!

"Growing up, my brother was always the one in the spotlight and I liked that. It was like he was the entertainment for me."

Ariana, on her flamboyant brother Frankie, who is ten years' her senior, interview with Lizzy Goodman, *Billboard*, August 15, 2014.

“I’m a big nerd. I love *Lord of the Rings*. I love *Harry Potter*. I love scary movies. I love dinosaurs, science, aliens, ghosts.”

Ariana, on her passion for enjoying all things geeky in her down time, interview with Joe La Puma, *Complex*, November 5, 2013.

Ariana's name is inspired by Princess Oriana from the beloved *Felix the Cat* cartoon.

Ariana's mother, Joan, is a huge fan of the animated series and thought the name was beautiful and unique.

Indeed, how many Ariana's* do you know?

* The name "Ariana" is of Greek origin – from "Ariadne" – meaning "most holy".

> “My mom has always loved Halloween… We’ve always had a very weird, like, Addams Family sense of humour. My mom only dresses in black.”

Ariana, on her family’s enjoyment of the spooktacular, interview with Joe La Puma, *Complex*, November 5, 2013.

“

I’m still the same person I’ve been since I was four years old. Literally. Obviously, I’m a mature adult. But I’m still the same girl. I’m still Ariana from Boca who loves musical theatre, who loves her family, who loves the beach, who loves animals.

”

Ariana, on remaining the same no matter what she wears, what she does, or how much her music or fashion changes, interview with Craig McLean, *Daily Telegraph*, October 14, 2014.

"

When I was a child, the only two things I watched were horror movies and Judy Garland films.

"

Ariana, on the two opposite sides of her childhood obsessions that now influence her personality, interview with Mickey Rapkin, *Teen Vogue*, December 23, 2013.

"

I was so young, and my mom didn't want to leave me at the rehearsals alone. But you weren't allowed to have your parents there unless they were in the show. So my mom auditioned, which was the funniest thing that's ever happened in the history of the world!

"

Ariana, on gaining the role of Annie, aged eight, at the Little Palm Family Theatre and starring alongside her mother (who got cast as Daddy Warbucks' maid!), interview with Craig McLean, *Daily Telegraph*, October 14, 2014.

"

I was a messed-up little kid. I remember one night my dad came home late from work, and we all had skeleton makeup on our faces. He was like, 'Is this Halloween?' Nope, it's just another Wednesday in our house.

"

Ariana, on her life-less-ordinary childhood with her macabre family, interview with Chris Martins, *Billboard*, May 19, 2016.

“There was always this fascination with the macabre. My mom is goth. Her whole wardrobe is modelled after Cersei Lannister’s. I’m not kidding. I’m like, ‘Mom, why are you wearing epaulets? It’s Thanksgiving.’”

Ariana, on her mother’s love of the macabre, interview with Rob Haskell, Vogue, July 9, 2019.

"

I loved playing a character as it was sort of just taking a vacation from myself. I remember saying, 'Mommy, I never want this to end.'

"

Ariana, on performing as Annie (her first role) aged eight at the Little Palm Family Theatre and using musical theatre as her refuge from her parents' divorce, interview with Craig McLean, *Daily Telegraph*, October 14, 2014.

“

I grew up writing songs in my room on GarageBand, and I would make the beats just out of layering my vocals over and over again. Very Imogen Heap-inspired.

”

Ariana, on her engineering skills at an early age and her biggest musical inspiration, interview with Dan Hyman, *Elle*, August 22, 2013.

“I want to be a recording artist for my whole entire life. But Broadway is something I would come back to at any given moment. I love, love, love doing theatre.”

Ariana, on her love of theatre productions – the origins of her performance career, interview with Dan Hyman, *Elle*, August 22, 2013.

“

After *13*, I went to LA and I auditioned for *Victorious*. I loved Nickelodeon growing up and I wanted to audition for a Nickelodeon show as soon as I found out that they were doing them. I think that the Cat [Valentine] is a role that I was meant to play. There are roles that people are just right for and I think Cat is mine.

”

Ariana, on getting cast as Cat Valentine in Nickelodeon's *Victorious*, interview with Lauren Nostro, *Complex*, August 27, 2013.

Ariana's first taste of fame came when the singer was 15.

She was cast as cheerleader Charlotte for the musical *13*, which opened at the Bernard B. Jacobs Theatre on New York's Broadway on October 5, 2008.

The musical ran for 105 performances.

"I started on Broadway. And before that, I was waiting outside the *Jersey Boys* stage door with a Playbill and a Sharpie, begging for autographs."

Ariana, on her musical origins and love of the theatre, interview with Kyle Buchanan, *Cosmopolitan*, March 1, 2017.

> "I've always been attracted to and got joy by very gay things. I grew up in a very eccentric, interesting household, that was super gay even before we knew Frankie was gay."

Ariana, on her older brother Frankie kickstarting her passion for theatre, performance and musicals, interview with Craig McLean, *Daily Telegraph*, October 14, 2014.

"Once Frankie got into acting in musical theatre and dancing, my friends and I became huge musical-theatre geeks and we would go back and forth to New York whenever we had free weekends."

Ariana, on her older brother Frankie kickstarting her passion for theatre, performance and musicals, interview with Craig McLean, *Daily Telegraph*, October 14, 2014.

“

I learnt a lot from my Broadway experience, it was one of the most challenging things I will probably ever have to do in my entire life, because it was eight shows a week – live singing with really hard choreography – and the spontaneity, you don't know what's going to happen. The thrill of not knowing what's going to happen, trained me to be prepared for anything. It set me up to work really, really hard.

”

Ariana, on being a Broadway star in the musical *13* – at age 15, interview with Shalin Graves, *Coup de Main*, February 25, 2012.

"

I was just in the ensemble, I barely had any lines, but they gave me all the highest harmonies. I was belting my ass off the whole time! My favourite thing about doing *13* was that Jason Robert Brown, who wrote the score, loved to push people to their limits vocally and I loved that. My range expanded because of *13*.

"

Ariana, on getting cast for *13*, her first Broadway production at age 15, and exploring her four-octave voice, interview with Lauren Nostro, *Complex*, August 27, 2013.

"It's how I've always liked my hair. Picture me in fourth grade with a little half-up side-pony flopping around my head. It's what makes me comfortable, and I feel like there's a thousand different ways to do a ponytail. A million!"

Ariana, on her iconic ponytail, interview with Daniella Cohen, *Byrdie*, May 6, 2024.

"I don't feel much pressure to fit in. I never have. I've always just wanted to do my thing. I have really good friends and good family and if I don't fit in somewhere else, I fit in at home."

Ariana, on fitting in with a scene or trend, interview with Sowmya Krishnamurthy, *Rolling Stone*, September 11, 2013.

"I have a bunch of really dope friends I've known since elementary school. They think it's funny that people want to take pictures with me at Starbucks, because it's weird."

Ariana, on her hometown friends that keep her "healthy and humble", interview with Chris Martins, *Billboard*, May 19, 2016.

"I still feel like Ariana from Boca Raton who loves musical theatre and dogs. I'm just working now."

Ariana, on remaining unchanged or unfazed by her global fame and fortune, interview with Chris Martins, *Billboard*, May 19, 2016.

CHAPTER TWO

PONYTAIL PRINCESS

Ariana's desire to perform has always been her yellow brick road, a guiding path to unlock her own greatness.

It all began here, in her early teenage years. First, as she moved from the Sunshine State to the Big Apple to begin her Broadway career, aged just 15.

Then, a year later, Ari found herself in California, where she struck gold as the fun-loving and free-spirited Cat Valentine. The rest is, well, a work in progress...

"

I started in musicals because I wanted to sing. I never liked acting. I auditioned for TV to get a platform to get a record deal and then I fell in love with acting because it was fun. After I'm done playing Cat Valentine [on *Victorious* and *Sam & Cat*] I don't see myself doing much acting. Though I would do a scary movie or a musical, at any moment.

"

Ariana, on her motivations behind acting and her path for the future, interview with Joe La Puma, *Complex*, November 5, 2013.

“The thing that my friends say when they listen to *Sweetener* is, ‘This feels like the girl we hang out with.’ I wanted to make people feel really good when they listen to this album.”

Ariana, on her fourth album, *Sweetener*, interview with Troye Sivan, *Paper*, August 23, 2018.

"Being in the middle of Pharrell Williams and Max Martin, two of the best producers in the world, both involved in my album, is the craziest thing in the world to me. I feel like a princess. I feel like a true pop princess."

Ariana, on the writing and recording of her fourth album, *Sweetener*, interview with Troye Sivan, *Paper*, August 23, 2018.

"Music needs to make people feel hopeful and free and happy."

Ariana, about the lyrical themes and messages of her fourth album, *Sweetener*, interview with Giles Hattersley, *Vogue*, August 14, 2018.

“

I was 14 and I flew out to audition with Liz Gillies for *Victorious* and we were all very excited. We both got cast and it was the best news we could hear! We were young performers who just wanted to do this with our lives more than anything, and we got to and that was so beautiful.

”

Ariana, on passing her audition for *Victorious*, interview with Penn Badgley, *Podcrushed*, June 12, 2024.

"When I was making the album, I would start filming *Sam & Cat* at 6.30 in the morning and finish at 8.30 pm, then go to the studio till midnight and get home at 1am."

Ariana, on the out-of-work hours involved in making her debut album, *Yours Truly*, interview with Caroline Sullivan, *The Guardian*, November 14, 2013.

"When you're playing a zany character on a kids' show, people don't want to vilify you. They're a lot harder on pop artists – they're unafraid to hurt you."

Ariana, when asked about the difference between TV fame and pop celebrity, interview with Chris Martins, *Billboard*, May 19, 2016.

"I was adjusting to these new things – red carpets, and people wanting pictures with me, and people taking pictures of me when I didn't know they were being taken. There was a lot of weird superficial nonsense that sprouted from it that I definitely wasn't used to. It was very weird. I just really liked performing."

Ariana, on being cast as Cat Valentine in Nickelodeon's *Victorious*, aged 15, and her first experience of celebrity and fame, interview with Craig McLean, *Daily Telegraph*, October 14, 2014.

In 2010, Ariana joined the cast of Nickelodeon's *Victorious* as the goofy aspiring singer-actress, Cat Valentine.

The show was a huge success and ran for two years before a spin-off, *Sam & Cat*, was created to showcase the talents of Ariana and *iCarly's* Jennette McCurdy. The show ran for 35 episodes from 2013–14, before ending abruptly.

For the role of Cat Valentine, Ariana was asked to dye her hair red, while the rest of the cast were brunette.

“

Hard, hard, hard work! It’s very hard and it doesn’t come easily… and luck! You just have to be in the right place at the right time and work hard and be passionate about it. Never lose hope if you love something!

”

Ariana, on what it takes to become as successful as her, interview with Lauren Kelly, *She Knows*, August 8, 2012.

“

If you listen to the whole album you get to know my sound. You get to know Ariana.

”

Ariana, on her debut album, *Yours Truly*, interview with Joe La Puma, *Complex*, November 5, 2013.

“

It was geared toward kids and felt so inauthentic and fake. It was the worst moment of my life. For the video, they gave me a bad spray tan and put me in a princess dress and had me frolic around the street. The whole thing was straight out of Hell. I still have nightmares about it.

”

Ariana, on the video for her debut single, "Put Your Hearts Up" (2011) – a song she has since disowned, interview with Andy Greene, *Rolling Stone*, May 22, 2014.

“

If I could, I would not do anything else. I'd just be in the studio for my whole life. I would never go to parties, events and red carpets. I would rather just be in the studio for the whole time. I don't even care. Nobody has to know what I look like. I just want to make music.

”

Ariana, on her workaholic attitude towards writing, singing and recording her music, interview with Dan Hyman, *Elle*, August 22, 2013.

"

I love the fact that Cat's different. I don't want her to seem like the normal, stupid girl at school. I want to keep her endearing at the same time, because she is a bit flighty. I try to channel Betty White in *The Golden Girls*, so it's a challenge. But I love her.

"

Ariana, on what she loves most about playing the character of Cat Valentine on Nickelodeon's *Victorious*, interview with Shalin Graves, *Coup de Main*, February 25, 2012.

“

I’ve been on TV since I was little so there are lots of funny pictures to look back on and say: ‘What was I thinking?!’

”

Ariana, on outfit and fashion blunders, interview with Naomi Pike, *Vogue*, February 29, 2016.

"

I got to fall in love with these characters that we created and learn what it feels like to be so in a character that you can't separate yourself from it.

"

Ariana, on becoming Cat Valentine, her character in *Victorious*, interview with Penn Badgley, *Podcrushed*, June 12, 2024.

Over the years, across scores of performances on famous late night talk shows and sketch shows, Ariana has unleashed her impressive talent for pitch-perfect singing impersonations of several notable artists.

Stars such as Jennifer Lawrence, Céline Dion, Britney Spears, Whitney Houston, Rihanna and Shakira have all had the Ari treatment, with many of her impressions going viral on social media.

“

I wanted a fun video that looked like it was flirty and romantic, and I wanted the video to make people feel how the song makes me feel. It doesn’t look like a music video, it looks like I’m having a blast with a bunch of balloons by myself with a cute boy.

”

Ariana, on her first proper music video for "The Way" with Mac Miller, interview with Lauren Nostro, *Complex*, August 27, 2013.

“

My fans jumped on board right away; they were excited, because I think they knew that I loved to do music first and foremost the whole time.

”

Ariana, on her fans' reaction to her transitioning from actress to singer-songwriter, interview with Dan Hyman, *Elle*, August 22, 2013.

"A lot of people just want to be famous – I never wanted that. I just wanted to make music."

Ariana, on fame, interview with Simon Harper, *Clash* magazine, June 18, 2014.

"I like the idea of separating myself from my younger image in a gradual, authentic way – I don't really feel comfortable doing something out of control to convey my maturity, because it doesn't feel genuine to me."

Ariana, on transitioning from child actor to popstar without degrading or exploiting her image or body, interview with Simon Harper, *Clash* magazine, June 18, 2014.

"

When I started working on *Yours Truly*, my label hooked me up with all these incredible producers. It was an easy transition for me because I was open to it. It wasn't 'Oh, I don't want to work with these people. I want to write my own stuff.' It was like, 'This is cool because they're the best in the business, and they know what they're doing. They love the sound that I love, and we can do this together.'

"

Ariana, on her collaborations with other songwriters and producers on *Yours Truly*, interview with Dan Hyman, *Elle*, August 22, 2013.

"Obviously, my relationship to child acting has been changing. I'm reprocessing a lot of what the experience was like. I think that the environment needs to be made safer if kids are going to be acting. I think there should be therapists. I think there should be parents allowed to be wherever they want to be on kids' sets."

Ariana, on the downsides to child acting, in the wake of the "Dan Schneider scandal" in 2024, interview with Penn Badgley, *Podcrushed*, June 12, 2024.

"I've taken baby steps in expressing my sexuality in my imagery. I'm all the way there now, but I'm also 23, you know? I'm having fun with it and I don't think that makes me any less of a role model."

Ariana, on her increasingly playful and sensual approach to her photoshoots, interview with Kyle Buchanan, *Cosmopolitan*, March 1, 2017.

“

Since ‘The Way’ came out a lot has changed. I’ve been followed around by people with cameras, which is insane to me. I don’t really understand it; I never will. I’m not too comfortable with the whole celebrity thing, but I think I’m doing well with the music thing, and that’s what makes me happy.

”

Ariana, on adjusting to increased fame and celebrity, and the paparazzi, interview with Dan Hyman, *Elle*, August 22, 2013.

In 2019, *Time* named Ariana one of the "100 most influential people in the world" on their prestigious annual list.

In the magazine, the artist Troye Sivan called Ariana "the most real person I've met" and "an industry game changer".

"

I would never feel comfortable playing Cat with any other colour hair than red, but I also feel most comfortable being myself with brown hair. So I get to be myself when I have brown hair and then I get to be Cat when I have red hair! It's like a *Hannah Montana* life.

"

Ariana, on distinguishing between Cat Valentine and her real self, interview with *Seventeen* magazine, June 25, 2013.

“

I love Audrey Hepburn and Chanel. I’m super girly when it comes to fashion, but on the inside I’m only fascinated with dark, macabre and weird things.

”

Ariana, on her loves and fascinations, interview with Joe La Puma, *Complex*, November 5, 2013.

"

You know what, screw this, I'm gonna do what I've loved to do since I was a little girl and I'm gonna make R&B, happy music!

"

Ariana, on signing her first record deal at 17 but leaving after being unhappy with the direction of her career, interview with Lauren Nostro, *Complex*, August 27, 2013.

"Every time I put my hair up, it's like a surprise. I forget how much I love it, and then I tie it back and I'm like, 'I love this look!' Every time I tie it up is like the first time. It's like true love."

Ariana, on her iconic ponytail, interview with Daniella Cohen, *Byrdie*, May 6, 2024.

“

I could never properly explain the bond I have with my fans. They inspire me and I want to keep doing what I'm doing because of them. I love music and I love what I do, but seeing their response to my work is my favourite part of the job.

”

Ariana, on her relationship with her fans and keeping them happy, interview with Shalin Graves, *Coup de Main*, February 25, 2012.

"I'm really nothing like Cat Valentine – we're both girly, but that's about it. I'm very quiet; I don't like to go out and party."

Ariana, on being different to the character she played on *Victorious* and *Sam & Cat*, interview with *Seventeen* magazine, June 25, 2013.

“Without my fans I’d be nothing! They are the most supportive and loving people.”

Ariana, on her love for Arianators, interview with Naomi Pike, *Vogue*, February 29, 2016.

"It can be tough growing up in showbusiness, you know? A lot of kid stars end up doing drugs, or in jail, or pregnant or get caught looking at a donut they didn't pay for. Which, yes, was childish and stupid… but I think I'm in a place where I'm ready to be caught in a real adult scandal. What will my scandal be?"

Ariana, on her infamous "donut licking scandal" during her *Saturday Night Live* monologue, March 2016.

“

We have loved and adored and respected each other since before we even met, just because we were fans of each other’s talent. We weren’t ready at all, though, to be together. We both needed to experience some things, but the love has been there the whole time.

”

Ariana, on her professional and personal relationship with rapper Mac Miller, her first real love, interview with Kyle Buchanan, *Cosmopolitan*, March 1, 2017.

“

The public know me as Cat, so I think of *Yours Truly* as their introduction to Ariana.

”

Ariana, on her transition from Nickelodeon child actor to serious singer-songwriter with *Yours Truly*, interview with Joe La Puma, *Complex*, November 5, 2013.

"

When I recorded 'The Way' I was like a giddy idiot. I smiled the whole time I recorded the song. The minute I heard the song, I was like, 'Oh my God, this it. We found it. I'm dying. It has to come out in a month. It has to happen!' When it comes on the radio, I crash my car.

"

Ariana, on recording "The Way"*, her powerful, breakout single featuring Mac Miller, interview with Dan Hyman, *Elle*, August 22, 2013.

* It was Ariana's first song to make the *Billboard* Top Ten.

“

I'm a micromanaging workhorse. Absolutely an obsessive-compulsive workaholic. Even as an eight-year-old kid [performing in *Annie*], I didn't want to stop working. I wanted to do every single show. However many there were in a year, I was in every one, whether I was a chorus girl or the lead or doing the lighting.

”

Ariana, on her love of her work, interview with Lizzy Goodman, *Billboard*, August 15, 2014.

Top Ten Most-Watched Music Videos (on YouTube)

1. "Side To Side" (ft. Nicki Minaj) – 2.2 billion views
2. "Bang Bang" (Jessie J, ft. Ariana Grande, Nicki Minaj) – 2 billion views
3. "Problem" (ft. Iggy Azalea) – 1.4 billion views
4. "No Tears Left to Cry" – 1.2 billion views
5. "Break Free" (ft. Zedd) – 1.1 billion views
6. "Focus" – 1 billion views
7. "Into You" – 1 billion views
8. "Love Me Harder" (ft. The Weeknd) – 830 million views
9. "Dangerous Woman" – 730 million views
10. "The Way" (ft. Mac Miller) – 470 million views

“

My years filming *Victorious* were some of the happiest of my life and that cast is family to me.

”

Ariana, on the three years she spent playing Cat Valentine in *Victorious*, interview with *Seventeen* magazine, June 25, 2013.

“

I don’t see myself as sexy and I’m not comfortable being sexy and dressing sexy. I don’t see myself ever becoming a sex symbol.

”

Ariana, on never wanting to be considered a sex symbol, interview with Joe La Puma, *Complex*, November 5, 2013.

“

I didn’t see myself becoming a straight pop artist – everything I had done before was very heavily R&B influenced. Until I worked with Max Martin, I really didn’t have a full appreciation for pop music – so I have a full appreciation for pop music now that I didn’t before.

”

Ariana, on working with the world’s most successful pop-music songwriter and producer, Max Martin, for the album *My Everything*, interview with Shalin Graves, *Coup de Main*, June 20, 2014.

"

I never really saw myself as an actress, but when I started talking about wanting to make R&B music at 14, [music industry executives] were like, 'What the fuck would you sing about? This is never going to work. You should audition for some TV shows and build yourself a platform and get yourself out there, because you're funny and cute and you should do that until you're old enough to make the music you want to make.' So I did that. I booked a TV show [*Victorious*], and then I was like, 'OK, now can I make music?'

"

Ariana, on using *Victorious* as a platform to raise her profile so she could become a singer, and idol, interview with Giles Hattersley, *Vogue*, August 14, 2018.

“

Oh boy! It is crazy, crazy-crazy. It has been an amazing ride. Geez!

”

Ariana, on the three-year process of making her debut album, *Yours Truly*, interview with Shalin Graves, *Coup de Main*, June 20, 2014.

CHAPTER THREE

LOVE AND LOSS

No other artist in recent memory has had as much profound personal and professional tragedy as our Little Miss Sunshine.

But above it all, this strong, independent woman has kept her grace and her kindness, a testament to just how bright she shines…

"I have to be the luckiest girl in the world, and the unluckiest, for sure."

Ariana, on her professional and personal life as equal parts success and tragedy, interview with Giles Hattersley, *Vogue*, August 14, 2018.

“

Even at my most heartbroken or most pained moments of the past few years, there was so much kindness. There was so much love, there was so much honesty and transparency and respect. So even at the hardest moments of loss and the grief that you hear on some of the album, I tried to make sure that it was kind and giving credit for trying and for the goodness that there was.

”

Ariana, on the lyrical theme of gratitude and goodness on 2024's *Eternal Sunshine*, interview with Zach Sang, *Zach Sang Show*, February 27, 2024.

“

I’ve never looked at love as something that I need to complete me. I would like to be complete on my own first and fall in love with somebody who is also complete. You can still celebrate and be totally obsessed with each other, but I want to feel a hundred percent myself so that I can love that person better.

”

Ariana, on love and relationships, interview with Kyle Buchanan, *Cosmopolitan*, March 1, 2017.

“

He would always tell me to sing it in my concerts. He would always say, ‘You know what you should end with? "Over the Rainbow."’ And I never did it until that moment.

”

Ariana, on her now-legendary performance of "Over the Rainbow" at the One Love Manchester benefit concert explaining that her grandpa always encouraged her to sing it, interview with Katie Conner, *Elle*, July 11, 2018.

“

I think that the idea of the American Dream, of success bringing happiness, is very superficial. I think that happiness comes from a different place. I feel like people have more to offer than just being really successful.

”

Ariana, on the American Dream and success, interview with Simon Harper, *Clash* magazine, June 18, 2014.

“If I’m speaking out about something I’m passionate about, I’m willing to take the brunt for fighting for what I believe in. And my fellow women are definitely something that I will always be one of the first to speak up about.”

Ariana, on women’s issues and speaking up, interview with Carson Daly, *The Daly Download*, March 11, 2016.

“

Being a good role model is very important to me, but at the same time I would never tell my fans anything that wasn’t true. I would never say something just to be a good role model. I try to be as honest as possible.

”

Ariana, on being a role model, interview with Shalin Graves, *Coup de Main*, February 25, 2012.

"You have to make sure you want it for the right reasons. Make sure your head is on straight and make sure that you are strong, secure, and are surrounded by people who are going to support you and be there for you and help you when you feel down."

Ariana, on her aspirational career advice to other girls seeking to become successful singers, interview with Shalin Graves, *Coup de Main*, June 20, 2014.

"

You hear about these things. You see it on the news, you tweet the hashtag. It's happened before, and it'll happen again. It makes you sad, you think about it for a little, and then people move on. But experiencing something like that firsthand, you think of everything differently. Everything is different.

"

Ariana, on her PTSD and the aftermath of the 2017 Manchester terrorist bombing at her concert, interview with Katie Conner, *Elle*, July 11, 2018.

"

By no means was what we had perfect, but, fuck. He was the best person ever, and he didn't deserve the demons he had. I was the glue for such a long time, and I found myself becoming… less and less sticky. The pieces just started to float away.

"

Ariana, on her then ex-boyfriend, the beloved rapper Malcolm "Mac" Miller* and his personal "demons", interview with Rob Haskell, *Vogue*, August 14, 2018.

* Mac Miller died in September 2018 from an accidental drug overdose. He was 26.

“I’m scared of celebrating the beautiful things that have happened in my life because trauma tells me that they will be taken away from me.”

Ariana, on her inability to celebrate good things due to her perceived bad luck, interview with Giles Hattersley, *Vogue*, August 14, 2018.

"I'm terrified of looking straight into the camera. I see people on the other side of the lens and the whole judgmental world of pop culture waiting with their pitchforks and torches. At the end of the day I don't care what they have to say, but knowing that every little thing I do is documented is a lot of pressure."

Ariana, on being judged as a musical superstar, interview with Joe La Puma, *Complex*, November 5, 2013.

"

I'm proud that we were able to raise a lot of money with the intention of giving people a feeling of love or unity. But at the end of the day, it didn't bring anyone back. Everyone was like, 'Wow, look at this amazing thing', and I was like, 'What the fuck are you guys talking about?' We did the best we could, but on a totally real level, we did nothing. I'm sorry.

"

Ariana, on the 2017 Manchester One Love charity concert*, interview with Giles Hattersley, *Vogue*, August 14, 2018.

* The concert starred Ariana Grande, Stevie Wonder, Take That, Liam Gallagher, Justin Bieber, Katy Perry, Miley Cyrus and Coldplay. It raised more than $25 million in donations for the victims' families.

“

I was researching healing and PTSD and talking to therapists, and everyone was like, ‘You need a routine, a schedule’ and, of course, because I’m an extremist, I’m like, ‘OK, I’ll go on tour!’

”

Ariana, on deciding how best to tackle her grief from the 2017 Manchester terrorist attack and the end of her engagement to Pete Davison, interview with Giles Hattersley, *Vogue*, August 14, 2018.

“

I don’t feel comfortable flaunting my body that much yet. I don’t need to do that to show I’m grown up. I don’t want people to talk about my choices or how little I’m wearing. I just want the conversation to be about the music and what I’m creating.

”

Ariana, on not wanting to be a sex symbol to sell her music as she transitions from child actor to serious singer-songwriter, interview with Joe La Puma, *Complex*, November 5, 2013.

"It's hard to sing songs that are about wounds that are so fresh… these songs to me really do represent some heavy shit."

Ariana, on the serious lyrical themes of her fourth album, *Sweetener**, interview with Giles Hattersley, *Vogue*, August 14, 2018.

* The Grammy-award winning album *Sweetener* is considered the first of Ariana's albums where she is the principal songwriter.

"

I took a selfie and everybody was like 'There's a big black dildo on the floor.' I was like, 'Are you kidding me?' People have too much damn time on their hands and just need Jesus if you ask me. I hope they find something better to do with their time.

"

Ariana, when asked "What's been the most ridiculous thing to happen to you on social media?" and the famous selfie that nearly broke the internet*, interview with Joe La Puma, *Complex,* November 5, 2013.

* The "dildo" was in fact a microphone for Ariana's looping machine, "because I'm a singer."

“

This old soul has been around the block a million times.

”

Ariana, on the wild ride that has been her life in the eye of the media since 2008*, interview with Giles Hattersley, *Vogue*, August 14, 2018.

* From 2015 to 2020, Ariana endured the death of her ex-boyfriend, the 2017 Manchester terrorist attack, a failed engagement to Pete Davison and the "donut" scandal.

“Love comes in many different forms. You can love somebody and not be in love with them. They can break your heart and you can cry over it but still not be in love with them. Love is a really peculiar thing. I think as far as being in love, I’ve experienced it.”

Ariana, on love, interview with Joe La Puma, *Complex*, November 5, 2013.

“I’m the happiest I’ve ever been.”

Ariana, during her relationship with comedian and actor Pete Davison, interview with Troye Sivan, *Paper*, August 23, 2018.

"

You know those things where you love something but you don't know why, or you're scared of something but you don't know why? I feel like all of those things are from another life.

"

Ariana, on her "past-life" informing her fears and passions in her present life, interview with Lizzy Goodman, *Billboard*, August 15, 2014.

“

I thought with time, and therapy, and writing, and pouring my heart out, and talking to my friends and family that it would be easier to talk about, but it's still so hard to find the words. When you're so close to something so tragic and terrifying and opposite of what music and concerts are supposed to be, it kind of leaves you without any ground beneath your feet.

”

Ariana, about her PTSD following the 2017 Manchester terrorist bombing at her concert, interview with Katie Conner, *Elle*, July 11, 2018.

"

Love, for me, is laughter, respect, good conversation, genuine support, and more laughter.

"

Ariana, on her perfect version of love, interview with Sharon Clott Kanter, *InStyle*, September 29, 2015.

> “I met Pete, and it was an amazing distraction. It was frivolous and fun and insane and highly unrealistic, and I loved him. But I didn’t know him.”

Ariana, on her headline-grabbing six-month relationship and brief engagement to comedian and actor Pete Davison, interview with Giles Hattersley, *Vogue*, August 14, 2018.

“

My Arianators are very important to me because they lift me up when I feel down. They provide me with endless amounts of motivation and inspiration and strength to keep going. Simple things, like they make me laugh. They are also there for me on a very real level, like a family.

”

Ariana, on her inspiring fans – her Arianators, interview with Shalin Graves, *Coup de Main*, June 20, 2014.

"

Love is a really scary thing and you never know what's going to happen. It's one of the most beautiful things in life, but it's one of the most terrifying. It's worth the fear because you have more knowledge, and experience, you learn from people and you have memories.

"

Ariana, on love, interview with *Seventeen* magazine, June 25, 2013.

"Most of my favourite people in my life are gay. Whenever I see my friends get bullied, or my brother get hurt for his sexuality, I become a raging lunatic. When you see someone you love hurting, for such a superficial, bullshit reason, it's like, how small and spiritually unenlightened and dumb as fuck can a person be?"

Ariana, on homophobia and her brother, Frankie, interview with Ryan Murphy, *V Magazine*, September 2015.

“

When I put out *My Everything* and *Yours Truly*, those first two album cycles might as well kill you. It’s pretty much as close to dead as you’ll ever be, and I think a lot of people don’t realize how tough it is.

”

Ariana, on the stress and anxiety of the do-or-die success of an artist’s first two records, interview with Troye Sivan, *Paper*, August 23, 2018.

In ten years, Ariana has sold a staggering 90 million record across seven studio albums, each one a commercial and critical hit that has progressed Ariana's sound forward.

1. *Yours Truly* (2013)
2. *My Everything* (2014)
3. *Dangerous Woman* (2016)
4. *Sweetener* (2018)
5. *Thank U, Next* (2019)
6. *Positions* (2020)
7. *Eternal Sunshine* (2024)

This makes Ari one of the top 20 bestselling female artists of all time.

“

I’m a person who’s been through a lot and doesn’t know what to say about any of it to myself, let alone the world. I see myself onstage as this perfectly polished, great-at-my-job entertainer, and then in other situations I’m just this little basket-case puddle of figuring it out.

”

Ariana, on the public and personal perceptions of being Ariana Grande, interview with Giles Hattersley, *Vogue*, August 14, 2018.

"Everything that I was terrified to try and was absolutely positive I would hate, I tried."

Ariana, on her approach to recording her sophomore album, *My Everything* (2014), interview with Lizzy Goodman, *Billboard*, August 15, 2014.

"I have always loved England, but I've never seen a city or a country take something that portrays the absolute worst of humanity and turn it into something that portrays the best and the most beautiful. I don't think there are enough words to describe my love and adoration for the people of Manchester."

Ariana, on the 2017 Manchester terrorist attack and the One Love charity concert, interview with Giles Hattersley, *Vogue*, August 14, 2018.

May 22, 2017

The terrible day that a terrorist walked into the Manchester Arena, UK, following an Ariana Grande concert, and detonated a suicide bomb, murdering 22 young music fans. A further 500 people sustained injuries. It was the worst act of terrorism Britain had experienced in more than a decade.

Two weeks later, the One Love Manchester benefit concert was held to honour those that lost their lives. Following the attack, Ariana tweeted:

"Broken. From the bottom of my heart, I am so, so sorry. I don't have words."

“It’s a horrible situation that we’re dealing with right now as women. I feel bad for girls who go to school with a short skirt and are told that they’re ‘asking for it’ just because they like to show their legs.”

Ariana, on the toxic gender inequality of sexuality in modern culture, interview with Kyle Buchanan, *Cosmopolitan*, March 1, 2017.

“I always put everyone’s feelings before mine. It can be taxing emotionally and drain the shit out of me but I’ve learned how to balance that out and be a loving partner but also nourish myself. A lot of people forget about the whole self-love thing when they’re in love, and both are imperative.”

Ariana, on being a loving partner in relationships (and also to herself), interview with Kyle Buchanan, *Cosmopolitan*, March 1, 2017.

"

I've always had anxiety. But when I got home from the *Dangerous Woman* world tour it reached a very different, intense peak. It became physical and I felt like I was outside my body. Pharrell Williams told me, 'You have to write about it. You need to make this into music and get this shit out, and I promise it will heal you.' I did, and it's now one of the most important songs I'll ever write.

"

Ariana, on *Sweetener's* final track "Get Well Soon", about Ariana's PTSD and anxiety following the 2017 Manchester terrorist attack, interview with Troye Sivan, *Paper*, August 23, 2018.

"My anxiety has anxiety! I've always had anxiety. I've never really spoken about it because I thought everyone had it, but when I got home from the *Sweetener* world tour it was the most severe I think it's ever been."

Ariana, about her mental wellbeing and her severe anxiety, interview with Giles Hattersley, *Vogue*, August 14, 2018.

“The most important thing to do as an artist is to push yourself to try new things and show people that you are growing and just definitely take a risk and try something that you’re scared of.”

Ariana, on being fearless and experimental with her art, interview with Shalin Graves, *Coup de Main*, June 20, 2014.

CHAPTER FOUR

PITCH PERFECT

Famed for multi-octave singing talents, Ariana is also a gifted and prolific songwriter, crafting lyrics, harmonies and melodies that have now soundtracked the millennial generation.

Equal in strength to her music, Ariana also has a reputation for not taking herself too seriously and is capable of using her loud Italian voice to spread lightness, positivity, wisdom, kindness and humour…

"

If I complained about being compared to the greatest vocalist who ever lived, I would be a very dumb, ungrateful person. So I can't complain. It's a massive compliment.

"

Ariana, on the constant comparison to Mariah Carey, interview with Joe La Puma, *Complex*, November 5, 2013.

Light coloratura soprano!

Ariana's four-octave light coloratura soprano is a gift that puts her in a very classified and highly prestigious group of singers. Other non-classical four octave singers include:

1. Christina Aguilera
2. Mariah Carey (actually has five!)
3. Prince
4. Michael Jackson
5. Céline Dion
6. Beyoncé
7. Leona Lewis
8. Whitney Houston
9. Jill Scott
10. Freddie Mercury

"

There's a lot of noise when artists say anything about anything. But if I'm not going to say it, what's the fucking point of being here? Not everyone is going to agree with you, but that doesn't mean I'm just going to shut up and sing my songs. I'm also going to be a human being who cares about other human beings; to be an ally and use my privilege to help educate people.

"

Ariana, on speaking about issues that are close to her heart, regardless of the online hate she receives, interview with Katie Conner, *Elle*, July 11, 2018.

"I learned how to make my voice sound like I was belting and being loud without actually belting and being loud. The voice is expensive, and if you're spending it properly, you'll be able to keep spending it."

Ariana, on the singing techniques she learnt from studying multi-octave singers such as Whitey Houston and Céline Dion, interview with Giles Hattersley, *Vogue*, August 14, 2018.

"

Whenever I doubt myself or question choices I know in my gut are right – because other people are telling me other things – I'm like, 'What would that bad bitch Super Bunny do?' She helps me call the shots.

"

Ariana, on her Super Bunny alter-ego as seen on the Dangerous Woman album cover, in shiny black headgear with long ears, interview with Chris Martins, *Billboard*, May 19, 2016.

“

If you want to call me a diva I'll say, 'Cool.' Barbra Streisand is a diva; that's amazing. Céline Dion is a diva; thank you. But if you want to call me a bitch, that's not accurate. Because it's just not in my nature.

”

Ariana, on her "diva" reputation, interview with Craig McLean, *Daily Telegraph*, October 14, 2014.

"I love working with artists people don't expect me to work with."

Ariana, on confounding expectations with her album collaborators (of which there are a myriad!), interview with Chris Martins, *Billboard*, May 19, 2016.

“Never doubt yourselves or waste a second of your life. It’s too short, and you’re too special.”

Ariana, and her inspiring life philosophy, www.grammy.com.

“I am the first in line to make an absolute fool out of myself.”

Ariana, on not taking herself too seriously – and wearing that famous oversized chicken costume on *Jimmy Kimmel Live!*, interview with Mickey Rapkin, *Teen Vogue*, December 23, 2013.

“

Everybody that I’ve encountered in this industry – and that’s been pretty much everybody – has been so incredibly kind, welcoming and respectful. I can really only count on three fingers, people that I have met that have been less than gracious to me.

”

Ariana, on her experience of the music industry (and its bad reputation for exploiting young female singers), interview with Shalin Graves, *Coup de Main*, June 20, 2014.

“

If a woman decides to show her boobies for a photo shoot, she needs to be treated with the same awe and admiration [as a man]. I will say it until I’m an old-ass lady with my tits out at Whole Foods. I’ll be in the produce aisle, naked at 95, with a sensible ponytail, one strand of hair left on my head and a Chanel bow. Mark my words. See you there with my 95 dogs.

”

Ariana, on the double standards of expressing sexuality in the media between men and women, interview with Chris Martins, *Billboard*, May 19, 2016.

“Spiritual enlightenment and self-protection are more effective than drugs and alcohol. I can’t have much alcohol without becoming very, very silly.”

Ariana, on drugs and alcohol, interview with Craig McLean, *Daily Telegraph*, October 14, 2014.

"For the people that don't get what I do or like what I do, that's okay, I don't feel the need to try and explain myself to them. I got over it. I am going to spend my time being the best at what I do and not worrying about what those people will think of it. Because if I love it and my fans love it and my friends love it, then I am doing something right."

Ariana, on her online haters and critics, interview with Shalin Graves, *Coup de Main*, June 20, 2014.

"A lot of times, women are labelled as a bitch or a diva for having a vision and being strong and using their voice, and it's just not the case. You can be strong and be friendly. We don't have to be just one thing, you know? Women can love to read a book and have sex."

Ariana, on her reputation as a "diva", and gender double standards, interview with Kyle Buchanan, *Cosmopolitan*, March 1, 2017.

> “I think it’s important to speak up about issues that matter and I believe we all have a responsibility to use our voices to help make a difference.”

Ariana, on using her platform to raise her voice, interview with Naomi Pike, *Vogue*, February 29, 2016.

“A lot of women think of the stereotype that comes with the word ‘feminist’. But there’s not just one type of feminist. You can be a feminist who gets their hair and make up done, you can be a feminist who cuts their hair off and doesn’t wear any make up. Who has lots of sex or who doesn’t. There’s no limit.”

Ariana, on the fluidity of feminism, interview with Colin Crummy, *Grazia*, May 3, 2016.

"

It's an incredibly human album. But it's also touching on *Eternal Sunshine of the Spotless Mind**, so it's kind of a concept album, which I haven't done before. I don't want to put out a single before the album releases, because I'd like for it to be heard in one piece.

"

Ariana, on her album *Eternal Sunshine* (2024), interview with Zach Sang, *Zach Sang Show*, February 27, 2024.

* One of Ariana's favourite movies.

“

I was just so happy to be able to make fun of myself. If you think you’re laughing at me, I promise I laughed first.

”

Ariana, on her stint as host and guest for *Saturday Night Live* and mentioning her "Donutgate" scandal * in her monologue, interview with Chris Martins, *Billboard*, May 19, 2016.

* In 2015, Ariana was caught on video saying "I hate America" in a California donut shop after being angered by the supersize of the donuts. Before she left the shop, she licked a donut.

> "I hate drama. I love women in the industry. I'm a big fan of all my peers. That's why I don't look at anything on social media. I'm like, 'My song's out!' Then I run for the hills. 'Here's another picture of my dogs! Bye!'"

Ariana, on staying out of scuffles and beefs between her popstar friends on social media, interview with Chris Martins, *Billboard*, May 19, 2016.

“

Sweetener sounds so youthful and unassuming at first, but when you listen to the music you understand what it’s really about.

”

Ariana, about the lyrical themes and messages of her fourth album, *Sweetener*, interview with Giles Hattersley, *Vogue*, August 14, 2018.

Before deleting her Twitter account in 2021, Ariana had a prolific social media presence.

Today, Instagram is Ariana's main outlet for speaking with her fans, with more than 400 million* followers!

* The seventh most followed person on Instagram in the world, as of July 2024.

"

This will fulfil me. This is what I want to say right now. I'm coming into my own, I'm trusting myself. This song is a personal anthem saying that girls can do whatever they want.

"

Ariana, on the meaning behind one of her favourite songs, "Dangerous Woman", interview with Kyle Buchanan, *Cosmopolitan*, March 1, 2017.

"Get off the internet! Walk away from the computer, don't give them a platform to reach you – go do something valuable with your time. Every time you read something that upsets you, just walk away and do something else."

Ariana, and her message to her fans about online haters and trolls, interview with Shalin Graves, *Coup de Main*, June 20, 2014.

"I am tired of living in a world where women are mostly referred to as a man's past present or future property/possession. I'm tired of needing to be linked to a guy. I'm not Big Sean's ex, I'm not Niall Horan's new possible girl. I'm Ariana Grande. I do not belong to anyone but myself... and neither do you."

Ariana, on being more than just the men she dates, *The Sun*, June 8, 2015.

> “There’s a brunette, severed head with the driest expression of all time on her face. I feel like I relate to it.”

Ariana, on her favourite emoji, interview with Nolan Feeney, *Time*, August 26, 2014.

"I'm a big perfectionist. I'm trying to channel super-confident women like Alicia Keys, Mariah Carey and Beyoncé, because I realized that if you want something, you really have to go for it, just like they do."

Ariana, on taking three years to record and perfect her debut album *Yours Truly*, interview with *Seventeen* magazine, June 25, 2013.

“You can’t let a 12-year-old in Minnesota ruin your day. They don’t know you and they never will.”

Ariana, on her online haters and trolls, interview with Mickey Rapkin, *Teen Vogue*, December 23, 2013.

“Honestly, I wasn’t expecting it to become a thing. I wasn’t expecting to ever have a signature look. But it became one! It’s just what I’m comfortable with and what works for me. I had to dye my hair red for a TV show when I was younger, but before that I always had my hair half-up and half-down in a ponytail. It’s how I’ve been comfortable since I was 12 years old.”

Ariana, on her now-iconic ponytail, interview with Ryan Murphy, *V Magazine*, September 2015.

Arianators*

The collective noun used to describe the loyal legion of Ariana Grande fans around the world.

Are you an Arianator?

* In October 2020, Ariana claimed to dislike the name for her fans. She tweeted: "Thank you to the most loving, incredible fanbase of all time with the ugliest fandom name ever created. Seriously, no thank yous for whoever coined the phrase 'Arianators'. You get no thank you. Just kidding. Love you all."

“Meditation like clears my mind… but I feel like it’s also hard work because it’s hard for me to clear my mind.”

Ariana, on how she likes to relax (when she gets the chance to do so), interview with Sharon Clott Kanter, *InStyle*, September 29, 2015.

“I feel like *Dangerous Woman* was a grown-up *My Everything*, and *Sweetener* is a grown-up *Yours Truly*. And with all due respect to *My Everything* and *Dangerous Woman*, I feel like I played the game a lot on those two albums. I wanted to make dope records that would put me in a place where I could then make whatever the fuck I wanted, but my favourite songs from those albums are not the singles. Like at all.”

Ariana, on "playing the game" (producing sure-fire pop hits) while making *My Everything* and *Dangerous Woman*, interview with Troye Sivan, *Paper*, August 23, 2018.

In 2019, Ariana won her first ever Grammy, perhaps the most sought-after award a US artist can achieve.

Her album *Sweetener* won Best Pop Vocal. It's safe to say it won't be her last...

“The planets, the stars, there's nothing more humbling than that shit. We get so stressed about little things when, in the big picture, we're just a speck of dust on this tiny planet in this enormous solar system that is also a speck in a huge, mysterious black hole situation, and we don't even know what it is! Thinking about how small we are, it's crazy. We are nothing.”

Ariana, and her intrusive, existentialist thoughts, interview with Katie Conner, *Elle*, July 11, 2018.

"I don't wake up in the morning and say, 'Hey, what can I do to shock people today?' I just think, 'Okay, let's go make music.'"

Ariana, on the media's dishonest representation in order to fuel continued interest in her, interview with Simon Harper, *Clash* magazine, June 18, 2014.

“

I have to walk this line between being 100 per cent myself and authentic with my fans, and being real, upfront and truthful with them. Because they, to me, are my friends.

”

Ariana, on her relationship with her devoted legion of fans, interview with Troye Sivan, *Paper*, August 23, 2018.

“I can text Madonna!”

Ariana, on becoming so successful she has Madonna in her phone contacts, interview with Davina McCall, *An Evening with Ariana Grande*, November 1, 2018.

CHAPTER

FIVE

LITTLE MISS SUNSHINE

Ariana Grande is pop culture's paradigm-shifting paradox.

She's a petite princess with a large heart; a kind soul with a loud voice, a good girl with a taste for bad boys, and a Little Miss Sunshine with a dark, macabre mind.

Who she becomes next is anyone's guess, but we'll be waiting…

“What you see is what you get. I’m honest, I’m authentic. I keep it real, because who the fuck cares?”

Ariana, keeping it real for her fans, interview with Troye Sivan, *Paper*, August 23, 2018.

“Sometimes people can confuse my niceness for weakness in a way – or ditziness or stupidity. But they shouldn’t.”

Ariana, on common misconceptions of her because she is "kind, friendly and smiley", interview with Nolan Feeney, *Time*, August 26, 2014.

“

I think people see me as a little cutesy thing. But I’m literally the most sardonic person you’ve ever met.

”

Ariana, on misconceptions about her personality, interview with Lizzy Goodman, *Billboard*, August 15, 2014.

“

Saturday Night Live (SNL) was the most fun I’ve ever had in my entire life. I love being able to make fun of myself. I love being able to put on a different mask. Making people laugh and feel like they don’t have to take everything so seriously is fulfilling to me.

”

Ariana, on her now-iconic appearance as host and musical guest of *SNL* in March 2016, interview with Kyle Buchanan, *Cosmopolitan*, March 1, 2017.

“I learned so much from Glinda and through Glinda. It actually helped me heal a lot of my own personal weird stuff that I had with being an artist and my persona. Having so much time with a character instead of a caricature-ized version of myself, it was really nice.”

Ariana, on Glinda the Good Witch, from the 2024 fantasy movie *Wicked,* as inspiration to contemplate her own life, interview with Zach Sang, *Zach Sang Show*, February 27, 2024.

“It’s sexy, playful, and sweet, just like me.”

Ariana, on her fragrance, Ari*, interview with Sharon Clott Kanter, *InStyle*, September 29, 2015.

* "I feel my sexiest when I smell good and I really wanted to give my fans a piece of me – my own favourite smell," Ariana has said about her perfume. FYI, it smells of crispy pear, pink grapefruit and raspberry, alongside rose buds, lily of the valley and vanilla orchids.

"

I don't know why people are so shocked by my swearing. I guess it's because of the character I played so long being such a goody two-shoes.

"

Ariana, on her love of cursing, because "I'm Italian!", interview with Nolan Feeney, *Time*, August 26, 2014.

“

I’m not like a little robot at all. I’m a real person. I don’t try to do things because they will look a certain way. I try to keep it real with my fans.

”

Ariana, on common misconceptions about her keeping it real for Arianators, interview with Mickey Rapkin, Teen *Vogue*, December 23, 2013.

“

I’m a good person – and I have a cute booty.

”

Ariana, on the fact that “giving, loving women” should not be “lessened” for showing their booty in a music video, interview with Kyle Buchanan, *Cosmopolitan*, March 1, 2017.

“There’s nothing, I swear on my life, more rewarding than seeing sweet little gays in the audience moving along to my choreography, or meeting a drag queen with like a 40-pound ponytail and thigh-high boots. It makes my heart scream. It’s the best reward.”

Ariana, on her LGBTQ community of fans, interview with Troye Sivan, *Paper*, August 23, 2018.

“

I didn’t care about the business part of my career for a very long time. I was just burying myself in the music and being like, ‘Wake me up when I have to sing.’ Now I can confidently say that I run my show entirely from top to bottom.

”

Ariana, on taking control of both the creative and business sides of her career, interview with Kyle Buchanan, *Cosmopolitan*, March 1, 2017.

“The secret? I rely on a really good brush and lots of hairspray.”

Ariana, on the secret to what makes her signature ponytail look so iconic, interview with Naomi Pike, *Vogue*, February 29, 2016.

“

I don’t go online when I’m dealing with shit. This is a very amazing time in my life, but also the most stressful. I’m adjusting and I’m learning, but I’m a lot shier than people think.

”

Ariana, on the pitfalls of social media as she starts her music career – and the online negativity she experiences, interview with Mickey Rapkin, *Teen Vogue*, December 23, 2013.

“

I have never wanted something as badly as I did this.

”

Ariana, on auditioning for the "dream" role of Glinda the Good Witch for the 2024 fantasy movie *Wicked*, interview with Zach Sang, *Zach Sang Show*, February 27, 2024.

“

I have the sense of humour of a 14-year-old boy. It’s very crude. When I was seven years old, my mom took me to see *The Rocky Horror Picture Show*. That’s just how my family is. We love raunchy humour.

”

Ariana, on her love of crude humour, interview with Nolan Feeney, *Time*, August 26, 2014.

105 billion

The total number of streams amassed since Ariana's debut album, *Yours Truly,* dropped in 2013.

This makes her the second most streamed female artist ever, behind Taylor Swift.

“I feel my coziest when I’m wearing yoga leggings and slippers and a crop top and a hoodie with my fragrance on because it smells really good. I love snuggling up and watching movies, writing in my journal, and watching something good on TV, like *American Horror Story*.”

Ariana, on what she likes to do on a day off, interview with Sharon Clott Kanter, *InStyle*, September 29, 2015.

> I'm proud of myself for keeping that cute shot of my booty in the 'Dangerous Woman' video. There was a moment when we were editing I told the director, 'When I am 95, that shot is going to be framed over my fireplace.'

Ariana, on the "Dangerous Woman" video shoot and the famous frame of her buttocks, interview with Kyle Buchanan, *Cosmopolitan*, March 1, 2017.

“

I go out in jeans and a hoodie every day. That’s what I’m comfortable in. But I do want to be a fashionista. But I feel like I haven’t really had the time to actually be a fashionista yet.

”

Ariana, on her fashion sense, and inspirations to inspire others’ fashion, interview with Dan Hyman, *Elle*, August 22, 2013.